Bliss Factor

By Johnny Perez

Table of Contents

Introduction Pg. 3

Chp.1 Jekyll Island Pg. 7

Chp. 2 The Faults of our Economy Pg. 14

Chp. 3 Consumer Influences Pg. Pg. 23

Chp. 4 Taxes the Necessary Evil Pg. 28

Chp. 5 The Ignorant, Lazy and Distracted Pg. 33

Chp. 6 The False Bull Market, Higher Learning Pg. 39

Chp. 7 The Diminishing Rights and Privacy of the People Pg. 46

Chp.8 The Secret Told Pg. 57

Chp. 9 The End Game Pg. 61

Bliss Factor source guide Pg. 65

Introduction
Bliss Factor

"Give me control of a nation's money and I care not who makes the laws."

Mayer Amschel Rothschild

It is no secret that the rich become richer every year. It is said that the 1% of the wealthy Americans (entrepreneurs, CEOs, accredited investors, etc.) make 300 times more than the average worker per year, and that figure is rapidly growing.

There are many factors why this unsettling phenomenon is happening; however, there are two of which, I believe, to be the most weighing elements of the growing separation between classes. One reason is that the education of personal finances and investing knowledge is not taught in most school curriculum. Also, these subjects are not easily spoken about in the household, or considerably talked about in social circles. It seems that this type of subject, primarily because it deals with money on a personal level, is considered a "hands off or taboo" topics. This could be possibly due to the fact that people, in general, tend to be defensive and not willfully open about discussing their finances. This could be due to several reasons that may include: lack of knowledge, frustration because their finances are not in order, or they are not reaching the money benchmark they previously wanted.

Currently, around 55% of Americans are investing in the stock market through 401k, mutual funds, buying stocks, et cetera, and most accounts do not have an amount that could sustain the cost of living needs during retirement. Thanks to the stock market crash of 2008-2009, most of Americans cannot trust or rely on investing in the market since they were "burned" and lost most of their investment funds for retirement in the process.

This is a shame because now, since so many people left the market, it makes a way for the rich to invest more and get richer. Furthermore, the lower and middle class withdraw themselves in growing their wealth since they opt out of investing completely.

This takes me to my second point why the class gap is increasing. Fortunately for the rich, whatever business or investments they are in they can afford professionals that work with them every step of the way. These professionals provide support to ensure that the wealthy get the best returns with the lowest risk. They even work with their families in an "investment meeting" to ensure that every member of the family is on the same page, to confirm their private asset plan and ensure their wealth.

Although the rich, for the most part, are smart about their money and a majority of them would like to keep it that way; keep the wealth in the families. They see money in a different way than most of the middle and lower classes, the lower classes see money as something to spend and work for in a vicious cycle. This includes credit, consumer debt that keeps the lower classes under water and their personal finances indefinably. Although some may rely on government support that keeps them on a particular income level, there is little incentive to rise in the classes. Most of the lower classes have to work two to three jobs that have meager and insufficient income to survive. This scenario is called economic suppression. That is why so many people are frustrated, disgruntled, and confused about their future and their family's future. Most of them think that a winning lottery ticket will deliver them out of their current circumstance and give them a better life. Odds are it would not, and in some cases, it would make situations worse.

Meanwhile, the rich view money as an asset that continues to work for them. Most of them have the means to pay their bills (cost of living) and invest in whatever they chose simultaneously. This then increases their wealth for their endeavors. They also are aware of their spending habits and money objectives so that they will keep their personal finances in check. In addition, they usually have no problem talking about money to their peers to generate additional ideas on how to allocate their money, which then grows their money in a virtuous cycle.

These two key factors greatly contribute to the inequality of classes and continue the separation between the upper, middle and lower classes. Among other factors, such as government policies and regulation from the federal and state level, that also contributes to this growing concern.

According to the documentary "Inequality for all," this issue began in the 70's where the working wages flattened out and corporate compensation began to rise higher and higher. Emphasis was on higher education, while worker benefits started to decrease. This is what sparked a women working movement, where both parents had to hold a job to compensate the increasing cost of living and inflation with stagnant wages and benefits.

This bring us to current events, where the lower classes are taking a stance on the issues and starting to demand higher wages and benefits which corporations keep pushing down; sometimes decreasing the amounts for the benefit of their company and/or laying employees off. Then, in turn, the corporate executives proceeded to give themselves huge bonuses after the fact, which made the working community question their agenda. Certain corporations did the same thing during and after the wake of the great recession; the government bailed out big corporations that were "too big to fail" and in turn gave themselves huge bonuses on our dime.

Yes, this is a concern we cannot turn our head away from. We need to address this directly since the issues that are rising are only getting worst for the middle and lower classes.

In this book, I will explain how this all came to be and the mentality of each income class, and how the issues weigh in. Finally, I will explain what we can do in this situation and how these issues can possibly be reversed.

Chapter 1
1910 Jekyll Island

After the brink of a near financial collapse in 1907, a new financial direction needed to be introduced. The banker and the government, in those days, wanted some type of financial reform to possibly create a new world monetary system in the United States. This would be the solution and the problem of the current economy; it was the beginning of the Federal Reserve.

On a remote island off of the Georgian coast, most of America's financial elite were invited; it was rumored, that the likes of J P Morgan, The Rockefellers, and the Fair Childs were present for the inception of this economic creation. This meeting was hosted by a senator named Nelson Aldrich; later known as the Aldrich Plan.

It is said, that these Wall Street bankers and politicians devised a plan to create the first central bank in the United States. This central bank was initially established to assist the government and the economy; which would fund conflict and support the government (while making an attractive profit in the process). How would they do that? Well, let me first tell you how they crammed this Aldrich plan through Congress into its initiation; this I do believe, whole heartedly.

After the meeting at Jekyll Island, Senator Aldrich (like the name) wasted no time and brought the bill into Congress. Conveniently, at the time a majority of the house was away for the holiday, the Congress took a vote. To no surprise the bill was passed, and one hour later President Woodrow Wilson signed it in to place, immediately. A very peculiar turn of event took place in a matter of months; it goes to show how a motivated plan and perfect timing could take advantage of the system.

The Federal Reserve, despite their name, is far from being a government entity. They operate more like a bank corporation, tied into every major monetary transaction. For an example on how the Federal Reserve works, let's say that our government is planning to pass a declaration of war. Well, we would need to fund the endeavor since our current monetary system cannot support a conflict such as that. As a result, our government would go to the Federal Reserve for a "loan" of money, which is then given at a specific interest payable by the tax payer (sound familiar, it should). Then the Federal Reserve creates new influx of money in the economy and the war is funded.

Unfortunately, the government is not on the hook for this new money interest, like I said, the tax payers are. We would be paying on the loan and interest until the balance is compensated. That is the beauty of this system, it's like a person you know possibly a friend or a family member who is taking out a giant loan on your behalf. In turn, it puts you in debt for their personal endeavors, whether you agree or not...

The thing I don't like about the Federal Reserve is that they do not have any checks or balances of the affairs that they are involved in; since they don't answer to anyone. Just like a bank, they can basically call their own shots and make their own rules if they wanted to: with little to no consequences on their end. Fortunately, the Federal Reserve, looking beyond their current shenanigans, has acted in our countries best interest for the most part; after cases of economic crisis. Especially in the situation of the last Federal Chief, Ben Bernanke, who took the reins and potentially saved us from an economic collapse. He implemented a sustainable plan to bring our economy to stable levels and beyond, due to the economic stimulus.

In times of crisis, the Federal Reserve is somewhat our economic safety net; whether or not that this organization is a blessing or curse, is a sensitive matter. So, let us take a look deeper into the organization for the truth of the matter, whether they are friend or foe.

As I said earlier, they are a private entity that supplies our economy with new money; you would think that by doing that it would possibly boost our economy as a whole. Unfortunately, that is not the case, if they did that directly to the U.S. Treasury then that would be a true statement. Unfortunately, they go about the process in a completely different and absurd way. They actually give the money, which is a loan to the U.S. Treasury and is billed to: the tax payer, to major financial establishments such as Bank of America, Chase bank, Citi bank and have them dispense of the money as they will, which the interest is passed on to the consumer.

So to recap, The U.S. borrows the money from the Federal Reserve, which does not give the money to the U.S. Treasury (at an interest) but actually gives the money to all major banks for free. Furthermore, this transaction is billed to the U.S. Treasury and in turn, is paid by the tax payer at an interest. <u>So basically, the Tax payer is getting the short end of the stick because they are paying for money that they did not ask for, and are working to get taxed on the money at an interest</u>. Sounds very shady, but that is not all!

So you walk into a bank wanting to make a deposit of your pay check. Most people would think that when you make a deposit you actually have that much in the bank to take out; let's say you have $10,000 in the bank at the time. The bank, by law, needs to only hold 10% of your deposit in the bank at all times, that means only $1,000 of the money is actually there and most of the time other banks don't even have that. Wow! And this is actually a law?

Hopefully, this is an eye opener to anyone that fully trusts the monetary system and all its inner workings. Bankers, in general, need to generate a profit on their customer's money to create revenue but most banks go well beyond that. It is like making millions is not good enough? That is the world we live in, in which other organizations and individuals take advantage of the honest working class and act like it is something normal…

But, I digress.

Back to the creative confusion that might be our down fall, the Federal Reserve that loans the government money at the tax payer's expense. You have a hand full of wars that the U.S. mostly won. You would think that all that success would possibly trickle down to the average working individual, right? Especially, since we are sending our sons and daughter to the battle fields and paying for the bill to go to war. No, as this country's beliefs, policies and traditions the average "Joe" has to work for their piece of the American pie; even though all these unlawful and scandalous dealings are happening underneath our noses.

The sad part about the whole thing is that not too many people know about this, and if they did, they are not willing to join together to do anything about it because of one excuse or another. I believe this injustice should be investigated and questioned, if not punished. But, of course, our government is supposed to be all about the people's rights and would never do anything that would potentially harm the working class economy?

Let's turn focus on the housing bubble that all government organizations allowed corporations to write frivolous housing loans, such as Sub-Prime Mortgage Loans. These loans that continued to be unchecked until the bubble busted in 2008.

Not to mention, every day corporate Lobbyist slither their way into politicians offices and pursue them to support a bill or vote a certain way for the good of their company/corporation; no one else. How does that add up in supporting the people? It does not for the most part, only for the agenda of the companies, corporation, and special interest.

I apologize for the abrupt tangent but there are certain things that you need to understand in order to fully comprehend the magnitude of this economy and how we came to be where we are. Many people have lost millions of billions in the "Great Recession" and did not understand why. Many fellow Americans thought that contributions into their 401K plans and doing the right thing was the way to go for some sort of financial freedom in their retirement years. Thanks to the ever decreasing social security, many people in the generation X, baby boomers and later will possibly not see any of it; even though it is around 20% of the government's budget. Could we see this decrease dramatically or go away completely? I would definitely bet on that one.

According to the research of Town Hall Finance and the Wall Street Journal the pot of Social Security will not be sustainable in the decades to come. So, what are we supposed to do when that happens? It is surprising to me that most people in the middle and lower class rely on pensions from their former employer, the government or both. Now, if the economy goes through another recession or worse, do you really think these pensions, retirement accounts are going to be sustainable or even present if the government gets their hand on the account balances? In the corporate eye that would be the first thing to go this is why most corporations go through the 401K avenue to save them money in the long run; leaving the employee to invest in their future. In turn, this will leave their workers relying fully on faith that the 401K firms know what they are doing in terms of the fund that the worker invests in. The reason is that many do not have prior knowledge to invest successfully in the markets, so they leave it up to the 401K companies to invest for them such as: Fidelity, Merrill lynch, and Prudential, just to name a few. The same thing happens with other mutual fund retirement such as SEP or 403b for example.

Now do you think they actually have your best interest in mind as far as meeting your retirement goals and objectives? The answer is hopefully "yes" but many of them say they do and do a completely different thing. So, in this case, I would check your 401K plan and double check those fees that they like to tack on to your mutual funds (load fees, high percentage fees, or anything you do not understand). If the fund is greater than a 1% then it is time to pick another fund or another 401K company. The reason I say this is, is because this measly 1% is compounded and as your account grows, so does the fees to your 401K account. I would suggest to possibly putting your money in an IRA if you have the opportunity. A Roth IRA is the best way to go, but if you don't fall in the parameters of that plan because of income restriction, then go the traditional IRA.

So back to the pension issue. The government also has troubles keeping their finances in order as well. Speaking of the government debt and deficit, the fact of the matter is that this overspending is also unsustainable. Currently, as I write this and look at the real time debt clock roll on the national debt, it is over 19 Trillion dollars (fact: a trillion dollars is a $1,000 billion, and a billion is a $1,000 million) versus the money that is being taken in from the tax payer mostly is over $3 trillion dollars annually. I am no math expert, but when you have more money going out than money coming in eventually you will become insolvent and will be bankrupt.

To put it this way, I look at this scenario as such. You have a person that has debt, let's say because of credit card, a car loan and student loans. I'd say this is a pretty normal person with normal debt, but the fact that this person does not make enough money to cover the monthly bill charges. So, this person has to charge the bills on their credit card or take out a loan to cover the bills or worse a payday loan which has ridiculous interest versus a normal loan. This scenario in this person's personal finances cannot be sustainable for long and eventually they will have to file for bankruptcy if they do not get a handle on their bills; plus they need to make more than they are giving out to Visa, Toyota, and Sallie Mae/Navient.

This is humorous because that is the same situation the government is in, obviously at a much larger scale, of course. The sad part about it is that there is no end in sight and actually Congress is increasing our country's budget year after year. So, again I ask "how is this sustainable?" and "what can we do to reverse this or at least slow it down to reverse this?" Well, the best solution is the simplest and probably some, if not many experts, would probably disagree because they like being in debt. That is "live within your means, decrease going out and increase income" which is check your budget and cut unnecessary spending such as non-necessity items. After that, increase your income, which could be getting another job or making money off of your passion, or hobby for example. And this takes us back to the government debt, I believe the same solution but on a much greater and complex scale.

I understand that many United states citizens rely on the government for supporting them because they cannot make it without the funds that the government brings such as Social Security, welfare, disability, food stamps/EBT, et cetera, but unfortunately, this will all go away in one form or another; due to the government's lack of responsibility of their financial spending and budget maintenance. That is when the government goes belly up and takes away our retirement money. Hold on they can't do that? Well, they already are with the decrease in the military pensions, public retirements and the ever growing company based pensions which are taken that is supposed to be safeguarded by the unions.

It seems that common sense is not in play here since our government likes to kick the can down the road and pass the buck or $19 trillion to the next political agenda. But the truth of the matter is, if this political and monetary system is not checked and solutions are not adopted to decrease the national debt, then what we have to look forward to is a country wide bankruptcy; it will be worse than the great depression.

Chapter 2

The Faults of our Economy

The fault of the economy lies within itself. The theory of capitalism is that it would be a free market for all, and that all would prosper not just the wealthy and rich. But somewhere along the way, it seems that the greed of certain groups got the better of the capitalist scenario and began to acquire most wealth despite the inequality it would create. So how did this happen? Why are they doing this? For the answer we have to look at past events.

As I explained before, beginning from Jekyll Island was the start of the Federal Reserve that brought our country virtually unlimited supply of money for the agenda of the United States. Thanks to the tax payers and the ability to print money, literally, each and every time they wanted to. This instilled monetary swing in the economy, which started from the great depression to the great recession we have now. This was also the catalyst to what sparked up the greed, raising its ugly head in our economy.

The growing wealth of the prosperous, on the backs of the average tax payer, did not sky rocket until late 80's and 90's where a shift was occurring. This shift was in the form of market deregulation, outsourcing, the dwindling unions and the move from the pension retirement to the 401K program. These movements freed up company's profits and created a "tax safe haven" for their billions of dollars in pay and bonuses; usually because of layoffs that the money is kicked back to the executives of the underlining company, for example. As I will explain, these so called "kickbacks" or "bonuses" are usually rewards to the CEO for saving the company large sums of money, on top of their already inflated salaries. But don't get me wrong, I'm all for executives getting an increase amount of pay versus their employees, since they are the boss and they are supposed to look out for their employees.

Nonetheless, the fact that these same executives are accepting huge pay increases and monetary bonuses, due to the fact that they put out someone on the street for a bump in their pay is absolutely wrong. Plus, to go a step further and have these big financial executives give themselves millions of dollars in bonuses after the great recession which the tax payers bailed them out, is utterly ludicrous. In addition, to this day most of the banks that exercised reckless practices that created the housing bubble did not pay down there debt to the American public to date, and probably never will.

One of the headlines that I caught recently is that the U.S. Department of Justice, agreed to a deal with Goldman Sacks to pay 5 Billion in damages over the mortgage debacle. This for Goldman Sacks is a drop in the bucket since their company has over a $68 billion market capitalization a year. So, basically, this is literally a minuscule amount for them since it is less than 10% of the money they take in annually. Besides, after it is all said and done the $5 billion will be less than originally thought since the fine is broken up. It seems like one financial company dodged the bullet, but that is one in a long list of companies that have these "settlements" doctored up so that they seem to do some sort of penitence for their misdeed, to put it mildly. (Go to https://projects.propublica.org/bailout/list and see the list personally)

Basically, these banks can get away with miss practices, like Goldman Sacks. This is mostly derived from the 90's deregulation of the markets; which was a green light to enter a much more risky strategy of investing. That decade was a spring board which led to the tech and housing bubble mess, and created two market crashes as a result.

The mid 90's was the focal point of "Executive Compensation", which basically meant that executives from any company could deduct all their pay in the form of stock options for the sake of keeping all of their money; just as long as it was in the shares of the company. Meanwhile, their average worker's pay taxes upwards from 30%, depending on their income, versus their executive bosses who pay 15% or less because of something called capital gains tax. This is a ridiculous tax difference between the executives and their average workers; since the boss obviously gets paid more (millions more) but now pays less in tax. On top of that, most companies that have directors who utilize the executive compensation strategies also include a nice market benefit called dividends. Now, to all who don't know what dividends are, it is a form of reward to investors that hold particular stock for a certain amount of time. So, in addition, the top of executives getting bonuses in the form of stock options, also get a reward boost in the form of dividends. Not to mention, the stock prices that go up because that also weighs into the returns. Wow!

Now, this would all be somewhat digestible even though this makes the rich richer; however, there is another sinister plot that these executives utilize. The revolving door of the private sector to the government sector; what I mean is that executive directs similar industries such as Tyson foods and the FDA. These types of industries have a revolving door of executives to administrators and visa-versa to push their agenda for more profit to increase regardless of what police or regulations they have to manipulate.

In the case of Tyson foods, for an example, many lobbyist and executives held public offices in the government to influence policy or the lack there of to grow their profits at the expense of the product and the market; which are the chicken and the consumer. The result is horrible living conditions for the chickens (since they live in the dark most of their short lives and sit in their own crap) and the disease that spreads to the consumer when the company violates standard sanitation requirements. That is why you see consumers being rushed to the hospital because of E.coli poisoning and then companies like Tyson foods do a massive recall to cap the damage already done. This can also be said about the beef industry as well, looking at cows as meat for consuming than actually living beings and feeding them GMO grown corn to fatten them up on an irregular scale, therefore sending the meat to the plates of the consumer. (Check out Cowspiracy the video to get more information)

Trust me, I like a T-bone steak or a rotisserie chicken as much as the next guy, but to know and understand the intentional practices of these companies and the risk they associate the consumer with is not acceptable in any scale.

Unfortunately, this is not the only industry that utilizes these practices. The financial industry also follows these same types of practices in their own unique way. Because of this unnatural misdirection that places the economy into bear market, recession, and even could spark another depression. Case in point, the housing bubble, this was induced market inflation that everyone knows what happened next so; I will hit this point on later chapters.

So along with the industries I explained, there are many others that use the revolving door strategy to influence and control the industry as a whole. Many industries such as pharmaceutical, health care, education, oil & gas, securities and investments, electric utilities, air transports, telecoms services, insurances, human rights and non-profit institutions are just many examples of these tied in industries.

So basically, this means that the few people that have the influence and the power to manipulate their specific industries because of the revolving door strategy and the money that the industry brings in; which was previously stated through executive compensation, can in fact do what they want. So I hope you see the irony and the vicious cycle that has transformed our society and engulfs our community.

These facts directly lead to the spectacle some like to call the suppression and declining lower classes (the low, middle and some high classes to be exact) and the signs are apparent everywhere. From the 10% actual unemployment rate, to the number of people taking some form of living assistance such as welfare, Medicaid or unemployment, for example. Many of the majority of the population is getting a government hand out because the cost of living and their personal debt has gotten out of hand. It is a sad situation, but the fact of the matter is that the lack of managing personal finance mixed in with the agenda of the rich has created a tornado that overpowers everyone but benefits the ones that have most of the wealth. So where did this inequality start?

Well the income inequality has been an issue roughly starting around the 60's and 70's and began to take form in the 80's and beyond. Many, due to the markets deregulation policies (mostly stock markets, commodities, etc.), outsourcing jobs, and inflated tuition for college, decreasing unions and the loss of the gold standard for the most part.

If you ask your grandparents, or your parents, who were born in the 40's, 50's and 60's about how the economy was and how the standard of living was, you would probably get a pretty positive answer from them. That is because the cost of living was reasonable and the income from jobs were comparable toward the monthly bills they had to pay to make a living. Things were mostly pleasant in those days, where as the father would go to work every day and the mother would stay at home and take care of the household and children. Now I'm not saying that because I feel that this is what a family should consist of, which a mother or wife can go out and work for a living, and collect a great income. But, in those days, it worked well and everyone in the family was content, and life for the most part was comfortable and decent.

So, what happened to the good days of leave it to beaver? Well, a lot of things, in general, without getting into a lot of political and civil right issues during that era. The population and the economy were morphing into something that benefited the companies and corporations more than the people working for them. The cost of living increased so that the fathers had to work multiple jobs or the mother had to go out and get a job, as well as sacrificing the home quality for extra income. On the corporation's side, their influence in the government due to lobbying and influences in policies, turn the tide in increased their profits and decreased their costs. Either through low taxes, low cost labor, shareholder obligation et cetera, one big influence was outsourced jobs in another countries because the labor wages were so low in those regions. For example, they opened up a car manufacturing plant in Mexico versus here in Detroit, Michigan to save the company money to their bottom line.

The other major aspect of the income inequality was the markets deregulation and the ever increased influence of the shareholders in company and corporations. Since the companies or corporations value the shareholder over the average worker, because they felt that they had an obligation to the shareholder to increase profits in turn, increased the share price of the stock; which could be at the expense of the employees. Take for example, the decreased pension that your grandfather or father enjoyed because they worked for a company for a period of time and was awarded for their hard work throughout the years. Now that type of pension is nearly nonexistent, thanks to the companies swapping to the 401K program; since the pension program is only available mostly through union based companies. Unfortunately, that is going away as well…

The fact that not many people are keen on these particulars is appalling, as the rich in these situations take more influence and more power from their workers and the public, in general. Due to the fact, that they are the ones that has Washington's ear versus the average citizen that pays for the politicians salaries. On the other hand, it's not the only tool the rich has in the suppression of the lower classes; they also have knowledge dominance.

What do you mean by knowledge dominance? Well, let's start with our public school system, which is a good start. These school systems have taught us and our children everything from English to Science to Mathematics. However, the school systems outdated curriculum never teaches critical thought or how to handle one's personal finance. So, what did you really learn at school? Geometry and how to properly dissect a frog (both you will probably never do in the economy unless you're a scientist or related field), but never hit on real world situations and problems that would benefit someone in important aspects of life. Instead, they are preparing students for subjects they will probably never use in their life since most jobs only focus on a specific task at a time versus using English, Math and Science.

Hence, my point is that we are programmed in our adolescence, by our school systems, to perform and pass all these various subjects but are lacking in the skills we actually need to become successful in the real world; that is a true injustice for our children. But then again, what about college isn't that where our children get the necessary instruction to deal with life's issues? You would think that higher education would hit on these topics, since it is the last bit of education that our students would get before they go out to the real world and tackle life problems. Then again, in fact they ignore or increase the issue primarily through misdirection to set the college student up for failure; because of huge student debt loans and again lack of personal finance taught in curriculums. Not to mention, credit card and money loaners who want to take advantage of them, since they see them as a high value targets, because of their age and lack of financial knowledge.

Many people listen to Dave Ramsey's radio show and so do I. It is somewhat amusing because most, if not all, of his callers that are in mountains of debt are usually student loans, car loans, credit cards, or medical bills that are piled sky high with unrealistic interest on all of these debts. It tends to be just about every time, that it was because of impulse or they thought they had to do it this way; so they entrusted the loaners into non beneficial deals. It concerns me how people justify their habits usually on impulse and not just thinking the deal through, only to get stuck with a car loan that is 30%- 40% of someone's take home pay at a 5% interest or worse; which in turn, the car will depreciate in value once you drive it off the lot.

So basically, my point is that the income inequalities issues are the responsibility that falls on both sides of the spectrums but the lower classes (low to middle) get the short end of the stick in the end. This is due to the lack of beneficial education in the real world, and the growing suppression of the American workers because of companies and corporation's agenda to slash spending, increase revenue and raise shareholder's profits. Hence, when I say shareholders profit I'm not only including the average investor, which is a single stock and a mutual fund but I am including the CEOs, executives or chairpersons that get a handsome bonus every year on top of their inflated salaries; in the form of their own company's stock. Therefore, now you know why the shareholder is so influential, because they are the majority shareholder (owner of the company). I guess there is not much wrong with that unless you lay off a couple of thousand employees for that purpose. In addition, keeping these bonuses even after your companies get bailed out by the tax payer, just like the big financial banks have done; not very justified is it?

With that being said, the fact that the less than 10% of the population own 80% of the wealth in America and is rapidly climbing as the percent lowers. Basically, 90% of the population owns 20% then? No, not really, because their slice of the income pie is ever decreasing and unfortunately, the powers that be, know it. Just look up wealth inequality in America, shown on YouTube and you'll see the sobering statistics of wealth inequality first hand; which again, will worry you then possibly make you angry. The first questions that popped into my head were: Why are these rich people taking so much money and not redistributing the money to benefit all the classes? Why are they doing with the money that they are hording? The answer, I believe, is because money is power and they are sickened with this belief, they are using money to make more money to create power from money and they do not care if the lower classes get hurt in the process.

The belief has gotten so out of hand that now Washington is riddled with this issue (more now than before) holding sequesters and bipartisan gridlock with one another; meanwhile, not getting any worthwhile solutions or policy change out of it. Mainly because most of the politicians we voted for are in the pocket of the wealthy (the high classes that takes advantage of the system) thanks to whatever type of contributions they can get away with. It's almost nauseating to think about, that these elected officials we voted for is mostly not working in our best interests, but the interest of the wealthy. This opens up an array of different problems from decreasing social services to increasing cost of living, since the capital policies are what direct the market even though the rich that gain from the market influence the policies. You see the unfruitful cycle?

Apparently, not much will change unless there is something drastic done about our current economic situation from the capital to the public and private sectors. Staying on the course we are on is not the answer; so, it does not surprise me that candidates such as Donald Trump are elected to represent the presidential candidacy. Since, I think it is a public outcry for help to change things; but personally, I do not think that it is the answer to our problem as a whole. Especially, not from a president that has just as many bankruptcies as he has divorces in his life time career (sorry that was a cheap shot). But of course, people like an influential public figure; especially, if they have a "reality show" or "movie" showing them as a chief or someone that could take charge.

The fact of the matter is that the solutions does not lie within a single persons leadership, which most rely on the president to change their lives and are constantly disappointed. It will have to be the collective community to rise up and demand a reform on the issues that are hurting the low, middle classes and even some upper classes. Capitalism, is not a bad word, and capitalism works when everyone benefits from the hard work and income prosperity that is shared by all. Because of these issues, and probably more than I did not explain is the problem, that will take this economy in a nose dive scenario. This is not a world I want for my children.

As Robert Riech said in Inequality for all, "who is working in a way that improves the wellbeing of the American work force, and the answer is nobody!"

Chapter 3

Consumer Impacts

United we stand, divided we fall… or was it the other way around?

We the people have a lot more power influencing the economy than we know; consumer spending is the driving force of our markets. In a positive working economy which is called "The Virtuous Cycle"; the wheels of production turn to the tune of worker get wage increases, workers buy more, the companies hire more, tax revenue increase, Government investment more, productivity grows, economy expands, and worker are educated, which increases wages and so forth.

This type of economic model would show how a true and positive working economy can implement and achieve a growing and sustainable economic state. This is what many people thought would be the result of capitalism in the United States. The founding fathers of our great nation put together the building blocks to where our country could thrive and achieve many great goal and objectives through a positive economy. Which some may refer to as the "American Dream", everyone gets their fair slice of the pie so to speak, and the well-being of the American people are elevated to new heights, and everyone wins.

Unfortunately, now it is quite the opposite and going in a downward direction. So the opposite of a virtuous cycle would be a "The Vicious cycle"; the wheels of suppression turn to the unfortunate circumstance of lower wages, workers buy less, unemployment rises, tax revenue decreases, government cuts programs, deficit grows, and workers are less educated, which keeps employees in low wages. Does that sound familiar? It should because that is what our country is currently going through. Even though the vicious cycle doesn't seem so vicious for the majority of the population mainly because our leaders and politician like to put on a good face and kick the budget, I mean can, down the road.

The proof is defiantly in the pudding; aside from our countries 19 trillion in national debt, our government is apparently doing what it can to save numerous government programs such as welfare and disability. But on the other hand continuing to spend and increase the budget every chance they get. Earlier I explained why this will not work in the simple's terms and yet our politicians just don't get the point, or they just don't care. Either way, it is a very bad situation for our economy to be in, especially after the great recession of 2008, which we are still feeling the effects of.

The situation is because the stagnation of the economy creates a perpetual down ward spiral because of decrease consumer confidence in the markets and in the economy. This is a direct relation to decrease spending and hording of money. Decrease spending leads to the deficit growing that leads to government cutting programs and so on and so forth. Obviously though this downward spiral no one wins in this negative scenario and will only stop when markets and the economy hits rock bottom. So how do we stop the Vicious Cycle before we hit bottom?

Well first as I stated before, the national budget has to be made sustainable. So **First** basically, all of the politicians have to stop their addiction of overspending and move toward the creation of a surplus in revenue. **Second,** employment has to increase as unemployment benefits decrease, where at the same time company's pay a fair wage to their workers so that the quality of live increases, which would be pay that is well above the minimum wage. **Third,** consumer confidence has to make a comeback and in a major way, big ticket items such as houses, cars, boats, etc. have to make a significant return, mostly through financing and borrowing on the loan to make these purchases. **Fourth,** some type of Non artificial economic momentum has to take place in the economy to possibly jump start The Virtuous Cycle but this is only when the first three steps happen.

Well since the government doesn't want to stop their addicted spending anytime soon, let us explore the other possible step to potentially start the wheels of the economy in the right direction jump starting the virtuous cycle. Obviously, if employment is to rise, then there has to be an increase in spending across the board mostly from consumers, but also spending from the private and public sectors of small to large businesses that supports employment would rise.

So as I stated before in step four, there has to be a non-artificial economic momentum to strike the current drive and reverse it. So what is this non artificial event? Your guess is as good as mine, since congress does not what to manage their budget spending. And the Federal Reserve's idea was to bring stimulus in the form of new money called "Quantitative Easing" to the economy. The strategy would seem to slowly raise the economy in an artificial sense and boost the momentum, but in the long run does not create a long term solution. They would not continue with this Quantitative Easing strategy since the influx of new money could create an inflation issue.

That is why the market and the economy are starting to feel a plateau of sorts because of the drive from the QE is starting to lose momentum. That would explain why the indices such as the Dow and the standard and Poor are beginning to breach a ceiling despite reaching new highs, since to date the Dow is breaching 18K and the S& P is a tad over 2100 in 2016. The momentum will not continue unfortunately unless there is a significant boost in the economy as a whole.

One thing I'd like to share is that if you look at earning reports for particular companies; they beat estimates quarter after quarter even though their business finances profits are the same or even lower. Sounds funny right? Well because it is, one of the market driving forces that makes the indices go higher is that their earning beat wall street estimates, which would give a good indication of how the economy is doing in that particular industry or sector. But unfortunately, companies are potentially inflating their numbers a widely used strategy that should sound familiar if you follow the stock market and that is through "buy backs." The company makes an initial buy back of their own stock and artificially raises their profits to beat Wall Street expectations. Not exactly sure when this strategy was adopted, but the growing number of companies that utilize this is increasing. In addition to that, most companies that are traded on Wall Street use a form of accounting, called Pro Forma, that is currently being investigated by the SEC since this type of account is a dumbed down version of their company's finances. The reason Pro forma accounting is such a bad accounting practices is because they leave out expenses that are either non-recurring or unusual transactions. Obviously this is a problem since businesses finances are not all cut and dry there are various dealing and situations that not going to be predictable or recurring.

So with these two factors involved contributing to the artificial increase of the stock market to the point that the top will eventually hit a ceiling, run out of steam and drop significantly. So this is one of the many issues of our stock market. So what does this point have to do with me?

Well I would like to say nothing and everyone can go on with their lives to do what is your passion and live long and be prosperous. But that is not the case, especially when it involves a lot of people's 401k retirements in the form of mutual funds. Because you can expect another market bust in the near future because of faulty accounting practices, this unfortunately involves working people's retirements. So not only is the game rigged but it is poise to make a lot of people's retirements poor again. Since in the whole scheme of thing if you know the basis of making money in the stock market you have to buy low and sell high correct. So that is why I believe that there are market bubbles that creates these special events for the people in the know, which are the wealthy and rich, since information is key especially in this situation.

The fact of the matter is that it creates another discounting scenario were the rich get richer and the poor stay poorer, because the few take advantage of these artificial significant events. And then the rich takes that money and invest in their own agenda via lobbyist, political influence and electoral contributions to push their schema even further.

But if this is new to your understanding than this information will probably blow you away. But the reason I'm writing this is to increase awareness and check our economic and political system since situations like this are happening all around the world of democratic countries in one form or another, even though the opposition would deny the this fact whole heartedly. Unfortunately, the wealthy and rich around the world have already figured out how to topple free market practicing countries.

On the other hand, the fascist and communist countries already have a handle on their population so it is not much of an issue to them since they have already accepted the fact that they are being overrun by their own government.

Chapter 4
Taxes: The Necessary Evil

From the beginning of civilization there have been taxes; from the days of the Egyptian Scribes traveled around the kingdom and collected goods to further the cause of the empire and the pharaoh.

Throughout history, from the Greeks to the Romans to the English Empire, they all have imposed taxation on their governing lands and territories. This practice is not uncommon for the citizens that reside in countries that flourish and prosper.

That is why it would be at no surprise that we would currently have to pay roughly a third of our paycheck to our federal government and, in some case, to our local state government with additions in-between like social security, Medicare, unemployment and liability insurance.

Taxes do have their use, of course, like paying for a bridge or resurfacing a road to avoid vehicle accidence; this all make sense and it should. This is what a democratic government working diligently to better the livelihood of their citizens should do. But the fact of the matter is that some, if not most of the government spending, are not going towards these programs that assist the working classes and are actually benefiting the wealthy and rich in many different ways.

The requirement to maintain social services such as Medicare, welfare and social security has been growing since the population has been increasing and the retirees such as the baby boomer generation have been collecting on their Social Security benefits. Along with maintaining our current standard of living to fund certain programs that should enrich our lives and increase the life quality.

I would say that our current tax system is arguable of being fair and just, but being taxed at more than 1/3 of a pay check is a bit over excessive. Especially when you have wealthy, like Warren Buffet and Mitt Romney, who pay less than 15% of their income and keep a majority of their capital. The amusing part is that they know it, whether they are utilizing their income through capital gains tax or exploiting tax exemptions, et cetera.

So this is what it is all about, and the game is to preserve your income and at the same time, degrade your outtake, and in the case of the rich it is through any means possible and anyway possible. The rich and wealthy are even taking it a step further and creating international tax havens in the form of company facilities overseas. How does this work? The tax haven overseas is being taken advantage of by many different corporations such as Apple, Microsoft, GE, Qualcomm, Wells Fargo, Goldman Sachs and Nike just to name some of the vast group listing (check out Citizens for tax justice website). It is all in the name of "capital preservation" so these types of companies take this loop hole and hide away as much money as they can in places like Ireland because their corporate tax rate is much lower, and in turn, these international countries economy reaps the benefits not the American public.

So, if anyone tried to pull something like that at a personal level, we would be in handcuffs quick, fast and in a hurry, thanks to the IRS. But since these companies are looked upon as corporations and exploit these types of loop holes, they get to enjoy preserving their capital with fewer taxes that hit their money. How is that fair? Obviously, it is not, but the government, since they screwed themselves because of this loop hole, have no choice but to let these companies utilize this type of corporate ambiguity because of their mistake; not being clear of their policy guidelines, it is similar to and works in addition to the executive compensation policy that was widely taken advantage of. So why don't they alter the laws to make these policies right? Unfortunately, there really is no reason for the government to modify or change these laws because, as I stated before, it is a haven for the rich and with the revolving door in place they can enjoy the same loophole and benefits that the wealthy and rich take advantage of; results in a loss and cripples our economy one dollar at a time.

The only thing that the Governments can do is to entice companies and corporations to bring their money back to the United States, and in turn, they won't charge the companies that utilized this loop hole the original corporate tax rate that other companies and corporations don't take advantage of; because they have some sort of conscience. I hear that if these companies bring their money back to the United States they will have to pay less than 10% corporate tax of the money to bring back to America. Wow, what a great deal! Even though these companies originated for the United States and had made their money from consumers and employees that work in this country; that made them billions of dollars to start.

These practices are almost as bad as the executive compensation policy and the revolving door strategy, because simply, it takes our money from taxes that were going to be paid and put to good use. Then we wonder about economic troubles of income inequality when strategies like this are being taken advantage of to further the wealth of certain groups, corporations and special interests.

I'm not sure about you, but as I am writing this I am starting to get heated over this growing paradigm, there has to be some type of end to this or the economy as a whole is in jeopardy. It really makes me not want to pay any taxes now, but it is a catch 22 because if you don't pay taxes, then there will be no assistance in government services and improvements right? Regrettably, these companies that take advantage of the tax haven and the executive compensation program are exploiting their hard earned riches to influence the economy. In this way, I believe they are working hard to find the next tax loop hole or the next compensation program to manipulate for their selfish schemes; despite hurting the public in general and creating despair in the classes.

But why wouldn't they? There really is no "force for good that will stop them, or force that looks out for the average citizen" so there is really no one that will put these select groups in check to right the wrong of the wealthy, influential and powerful. The reason I stated earlier is because they are all tied into the same game. Yes, even our government officials, they may put on a good face and say to the public "we are making efforts to making the laws fair for everyone, especially the lower classes." But in reality, the facts are quite the opposite and when a politician goes against the grain and puts up a worthwhile bill or policy that goes against the principles of the wealthy, it is when the bill gets shot down and usually it is in a major way so that anything after will not have a chance.

Often these politicians will deface the bill or policy, (and this is the funny but sickening part) they will gut the entire bill or policy and fill it with whatever they choose is relevant for their agenda, basically. They would fill the bill or policy with things that would have no relevance in the current bill trying to be passed. Just so that they would have a certain party vote or would have their support for the bill or policy. Unfortunately, it would defeat the purpose of the bill in the first place because it was changed so much that it did not hold the right point of the bill.

This particular injustice is not only happening in the Federal level, but is also happening on the state and local level as well; it is considered one of the politician's playbook strategies to mislead a bill that would actually make a lasting positive difference in the lives of the people. But of course, if it is remotely at the expense of capital coming from the rich. Well then, we just can't have that now, can we?

This disastrous situation reminds me of a story one of my co-workers who told me when I was working at a region retail food store. He was from Kazakhstan (one of those former Soviet countries) but he migrated to the

United States with his family and became a full fledged citizen. He told me that when he returns to his country (which is not too often) to see his other family, as soon as he steps off the plane he is greeted by some people outside of the airport or wherever. At first it seems like it is someone that is just being friendly to you and they start asking questions like "how your flight was or how America is?" Then they said "ok, so you give me $200, so I don't hurt your family." These people say this with a straight face… I was shocked when I heard this, but even though these counties are very corrupt in the way they do business, at least you know who is actually shaking you down for your money. Instead of the situation we have, where most people do not have a clue, because there is no face you can see that is a representation of the thug at the airport in Kazakhstan, and that is how they like it.

Everything is already set in place long ago to take a good portion of the wage you work for, and this all can be thanks to the ever present Internal Revenue Service, our politicians, our president and their efforts we have; however, there is no choice to pay our taxes and file a tax return every year even after knowing this information.

Chapter 5
The Distracted, Lazy and Ignorant

We can all agree that we have the best entertainment in the world: "World class amusement." From Hollywood's movies, to the amusement parks of California and Florida, to the sports we enjoy to gaming systems and music. Our entertainment is top notch and really I believe not many international countries can rival the leisure we enjoy today, because it takes a lot of money to pay these actors and athletes millions of millions of dollars just to entertain us.

The entertainment industry has brought in more than 2 trillion dollars since 2011, and is obviously growing exponentially. Names like Walt Disney, Time Warner, NFL and FOX are giants in this particular industry and their profits are actually increasing to topple numbers that were in 2007 before the crash. So it is no surprise that when times are good that this industry does very well for the most part. But, what you may not know is that this industry is governed by the media mostly, and the people that govern the media are in fact the same people that utilize these ambiguities for the rich. How is media governing the entertainment? Let me explain. We'll have to go back to the beginning of modern entertainment starting from the radio.

Back in the day, radio was the modern form of media in the 1900 till now, since we still utilize the air wave of radio to listen to our favorite program. In those days, radio was the way to get your daily fix of Lone Ranger, Amos and Andy, et cetera, from radio developed movies theaters and television. As the two became more accepted in the household, the television started to create more influence and thus began to affect communities homes and lives in general.

Which brings us to the current media situation we have today, almost every household has some form of media whether it is a T.V., computer, radio, and even a smart phone has the capabilities to put out the message of whatever is passed on through those means. So, if media is the single best form of communication to occupy a household and their community, then why wouldn't the rich want to manipulate it? I think most people already know the answer to that question and it obviously is a "yes, they do", this is the most influential method that they use to connect to the populous.

So it is not surprising that the quality of programming that is happening currently is mostly garbage from reality shows, to day time television; it seems if you watch them continuously you seem to lose some type of intelligence. Every time you watch the news, whether it is local, national or international, it is mostly negative sediment. Don't get me wrong some shows on T.V. are actually entertaining but unfortunately, a majority of them are sub quality programming (you know what I mean).

I don't really believe in the conspiracy that subliminal messages are coming out of our television, but I do believe that the scheme is to invade our positive mental state, distracting us and confuse our beliefs with all sorts of trash that do not pertain to our lives, and in most cases, do not weigh into our morals and values as a society. With that being said, these media influences weighs in on the moral fiber and opens us up to a demoralized community, especially when the programming tries to manipulate or spark up subjects such as race, gender, or sexual orientation. It seems that the powers that influence the media industry have to pick at these topics in order to create hate and discontent in the community and in turn, segregate certain groups or populations to turn against each other; or at least create a disgruntlement society.

You would think that a country of ours which is the leader in a lot of way around the world, wouldn't have these types of issues among our population, but I believe that because of the mix of our beliefs and old traditions that the media plays on, exploits and takes advantage, and in turn segregates us as a massed civilization. Kind of like a wound that has been injured a long time ago but still hurts because someone comes around and messes with it to re injure the wound; same principle.

This is not the only the way the wealthy get over, the food that we consume whether it is at the local supermarket or at a McDonald's restaurant down the street, in some form or another has tainted the consumer's food supply. The reason I say this, is because of the whole Genetically Modified Organism (GMO) issue, where the industry is manipulating our food supply through genetically modified corn and soy bean. Now, you would think that those two crops are really nothing to worry about, but the fact of the matter is that they are in almost every type of food you can think of and other that you didn't even know.

Take for example, the various foods that have some form of high fructose corn syrup in them, basically anything they would include in these products; from sweetener or even mixed into the food is unfortunately, in there. Regrettably, our current laws allow the GMO corn and soybean to be processed into these types of foods that we consume on a massive scale. The soy bean is also into a majority of our food products in the form of lecithin or food oils.

Those two vegetables control much the food supply that we consume on a daily basis; it is so ridiculous that the debate is brought up to where the FDA would not label such food to give the consumer information regarding the food they eat so that the consumer can make their own choices as to buy products that contain these types of ingredients. Companies like Monsanto's that engineer the GMO seed do not want this legislation to happen; because information is power the rich do not want that, which would check the balance of power.

Other issues are that companies like Monsanto try to corner the market and keep the farmer that grow their GMO corn or soy bean seed from keeping their seeds. If these farmers keep their seeds then there will be legal action taken against them, simply because the GMO seed has a patent on them, hence restricting the farmers from keeping the seed to replant, even though that would be practical and save everyone money. How is that justified? Why are they so adamant on destroying their own seeds? That is because it is property of that company which if the seed belongs to Monsanto and the seed would be their property, since they hold the rights to the patent that is granted by the government.

So, the GMO seed is the start of the poor quality of our food, since they are in everything that calls for the GMO type of food. Our meat supply is not safe as well; GMO corn is feed into our cows, pigs and chickens so that they can grow abnormally obese, along with pumping them up with other types of chemicals such as steroids to strangely develop the animals in an unnatural way; they can be fattened up for consumption. These animals basically cannot support their own weight to even stand upward because they are so malnourished and obese, which they live in their own feces from the time they are born to the time they get slaughtered.

This is a growing concern in this industry because the spread of diseases in the meat supply is prevalent but also in the corn and soy supply, as well. The food supply seems to get tainted since the feed somehow gets mixed in because of a corn processing plant which is next to a slaughter house. That is why you see vegetable that are in plastic packaging have diseased such as E. coli inside them or a young child gets sick off of eating a hamburger at a fast food restaurants.

The very thought of this out right disgusts me, since it is the lack of following guidelines from the FDA that creates the issues in the first place; when a company that is found guilty of a violation the companies get a slap on the wrist in the form of a small fine. Meanwhile, a mother and father grieve the lost of their child because of the lack of scrutiny from a butcher plant. How very shameful! But again, it is because the revolving door policies in these types of gridlock industries which the companies can get away with, and disregard regulations like this.

The fact that the public often chooses to go the cheap and easy route when it comes to food consumption and the fast food industry already knows this. For decades we have been hypnotized by the easy and low-priced food that the fast food industry provides to the consumer. They would not be in business if customers did not keep going back to these establishments for their Whoppers or Big Macs, so in a many ways we are the contributors to the dilemma when we go to Taco Bell or Burger King for a combo meal for five dollars.

Fortunately, we are starting to wake up and turn to more of an organic and natural food sources, that is why I commend restaurants and food stores such as Chipotle and Whole Foods that try to create a stand about what we put in our bodies and where we get the food sources from. These types of choices and alternatives need to be abundant to at least give the consumer a chance to eat right, live right with our morals and values in their proper place.

The choice to live GMO free and organically natural won't be easy because currently you will have to pay a bit more and you will have to be close to sources that support this life style but your body, your mind and your soul will thank you in the long run.

So, we hit on the distraction and the lazy portion but the ignorant is probably the most important aspect of the evil Triad because as you know, and I stated earlier, "knowledge is power," and what the public does not know will hurt them and make the rich richer. All three of these issues, I believe, feed on itself and make the momentum of being energized, focused, and aware to be productive society a very difficult mission. I believe, that is why we have so many people abusing our welfare and social service programs because they have all needed help and became content in the substandard life they are living. Not to mention problems such as drugs, domestic abuse, and any crime in-between can be manifested because of this type of living situation.

As I identified earlier, the lack of knowledge starts from our education beginnings in public schools, because they do not hit on real world issues.

Setting us up for a long road to certain disappointment, that is a real injustice on our society. The outcome is a misinformed adult that needs the government to support them.

For most of us, we were not raised to look forward to a trust fund from our rich parents, so everything we do, we do it with a lot of hard work and dedication. Unfortunately, in these days this is just not enough to be prosperous in life; evidently the game plan that involves a great financial plan and perseverance along with the right information will be the key to beating this current economic climate and to win with money. This is the challenge that we all face in the battle to meet a comfortable retirement. However, many of us do not reach that point because of life event happening, not budgeting correctly and not living within our means.

Not only is knowledge a contributing factoring into being financially successful but acting on a plan to steer in the right direction is necessary as well. As I state throughout this book even though I hit on a lot of negative issues, I also try to find viable solutions, despite the rich and wealthy's schemes to overwhelm the American population.

Chapter 6
The False Bull Market and Higher Education

When I say false bull market, I mean the artificial influences that manipulate the market in general, as I stated in previous chapters; lack of showing real numbers in accounting and not allowing the stocks to naturally make their moves are what makes these phony scenarios. I have been watching and investing in the market for more than 15 years and I still feel it is a great way to build wealth and a great way to get returns on invested money. But of course, if you are an abide follower of the stock market and Wall Street (which I watch CBNC/Bloomberg regularly), every so often you will see some strange happenings. Happenings such as "flash crashes" and "mini corrections" that throw investors off, when they thought they had the markets figured out.

Aside from that, the market creates bubbles that eventually burst and impact the vast majority of retirement savings accounts; like the housing market and the market crash of 2008. But, unfortunately, this is how I look at the basis of the market. Many powerful investors and hedge funds are most likely exercising the principle of buy low and sell high; that is the number one rule for anyone that wants to play their hand in the stock market, which of course is pretty simple to understand. So, let's say when influential investors are not making the amount of money they want to make (since billions are not enough), one of their strategies are to create bubbles; they can be small bubbles like small corrections or huge bubbles like the housing bubble.

This strategy mostly guarantees that they are the first to sell at the top and the first to buy at the bottom in the markets, since they are usually one of the few that know when this event is going to happen. For the huge bubbles, like the house bust, only a few knew the potential catastrophe that would happen because of sub prime lending and irresponsible business practices in the housing industry. Unfortunately for the public, everyone is tied into this particular bust one way or another and when one aspect of the market goes so does everything else (house of cards).

So, I understand this event as a grand conspiracy of sorts to syphon the majorities' money in the form of buying cheap stocks, commodities, and tangible assets (like properties) because the market had no choice and people lost their jobs in the process. Even though, currently, the indices are at fresh highs and even though most retirement accounts are almost back to the levels that they once were in 2008; it is still a preposterous turn of events that should never have happened at all. As a result to the finance companies that were tied into the bubble exercised shady business practices and expected the tax payers to bail them out.

In the movie "The Big Short," one of the scenes that astonished me was when Steve Carell and his team took a trip to Florida to get an idea on how the housing market environment was, and how they are still making money off of overpriced houses. In one part of the movie, the team entered a strip club and interviewed one of the strippers that had multiple homes; Steve Carell asked how they could loan money to her (not because she's a stripper). She owned five houses and one condo, some ridiculous number like that, in an adjustable rate mortgage, and her response was "they just keep giving me loans, so I keep financing them." He was dumbfounded and amazed of how that could be.

Throughout the movie, Steve and his team were trying to find any form of evidence to reverse the inevitable disaster that was eventually going to happen. He even tries to talk some sense into a CDO manager and the S & P director that contributed to the whole housing bubble but unfortunately, did not reply to any of his questions about the subject. Even with his Harvard education, the CDO manager could not see the oncoming dangers that were around the corner, but money and power seems to blind people from the realities of the truth. When times are good and the money continues to flow the public, in general, do not seem to care about the pending hazards ahead.

The Standard and Poor (S & P) rating system was in on the whole scheme as well, since they were supposed to be a reputable company; rating the quality of investment like bonds. An investment vehicle, like mortgage back securities, which are basically huge mortgage swaps from bank to bank in the form of a bonds or funds, was given the AAA rating even though they saw the mortgage defaults one after another and eventually were junk.

Now, thanks to the housing bubble, the confidence of the economy and the markets are a direct reflection of events in the past. However, if more people saw the warnings, took them seriously and did their own home work on the situations while possibly creating a contingency plan that could avoid all of the catastrophes, then maybe we wouldn't be in the mess we are today.

It just amazes me how blatant the situation is, yet everyone seems to be steering in the direction of the cliff. While everyone else in the herd blindly ignores the signs that gives the indication that there are some things ahead that will put us all in danger. But of course it is in our nature to forget about the bad times, when times are good; the party is still rolling.

Regrettably, there is sediment though that the great recession, which is still in the minds of the people, is what reflects consumer sediment or confidence. Now, I'm not saying go through life regarding finances constantly watching your back, but I am saying that we all need to have some sense of awareness. Do some due diligence, if times are too good there might be a problem. Because if times are too good, then that would be a good time to look at the signs and at least check it out; come up with a strategy to weather through the pending danger to come.

Just like Steve Carell and his team in "The Big Short," they basically put down trades that would short the market because they knew what was to come. They were deeply saddened that they had to do it because of the looming situation. However, it was a condition that if I knew now what would come about then, I would do the same because of others: stubbornness, lack of carefulness and stupidity. But what could they do? All the influential people that they tried to talk some sense into did not listen.

After the great recession, the public started to look for other avenues to try and get an advantage on their careers or just find a job that pays a lot better to get ahead. The answer was to go back to school and earn a degree, land a job that pays more than the job they had, or they got laid off and went back to school. Many people went to college and took out massive loans to support the tuition of these schools that had the classes and curriculum for a degree.

Depending on your degree focus and the school's tuition, loans could be from $30k to, I heard, $250k in debt; which could be a difference from a social worker, to a lawyer or a doctor. I, personally, don't think that a $250k in student loans can be justified; even though the loaner thinks "of course you'll land a great paying job," which is not guaranteed. This will only take you 20-30 years to pay off a private school loan, which is just about the same as taking out a mortgage loan but at a higher interest.

This is the new debt debacle that we face now; bogging students down that are recently new graduates, with student loans the size of their apartments or houses, in addition to their other debts such as car loan, credit cards, etc.

So, this will not surprise you, since so many people are in this type of horrible situation, that it would be tied into the rich and wealthy as well. Really, so how are they tied in? Well, they are not tied into all of the schools, fortunately, but they have big stakes. These are being exposed for what they are "For-Profit schools" or for "their" profit schools; on the outside they look great and desirable, but people learned that these schools lock their students into awful student loan deals and give substandard education, to boot. Actually, some of these schools are not even accredited; they just establish themselves as a respectable school and start taking student applications before anyone is the wiser.

Schools like Everest College, Kaplan, and University of Phoenix are just some of the colleges on the list that are in question about their enrollment practices, tuition and curriculum. Actually, as I write this Corinthian College, which runs Everest Institute, Wyotech and Heald College in their network of colleges, all had to close their door because of their shady business practices. One of the headlines on CNN money was "Corinthian is being sued by the Feds for the alleged predatory lending scheme, preying on low-income students, and falsely inflating job placement numbers." Not just Corinthian College is guilty of this, but a good portion of for profit colleges, because a majority of them are a factory producing students, to get in and graduate as fast as possible. A lot of these colleges are remote, meaning that you can take a class from another location where students mostly do their work from their homes because of their busy schedules.

This would be a great idea if all the for-profit schools followed the regulations and guidelines that involve accreditation and fair lending practices. But of course, if you're all about making money for your schools (for-profit company) and the shareholders (since schools like Corinthian college are traded on the stock market) and students are the last thing on the agenda, of course you will run into issues. That is why you don't see Harvard or Stanford have the same problems because they are dedicated to the students for a quality education, even though it is ridiculously difficult to get accepted into these establishments and the tuition is astronomical.

So, I want to share a story about my experience applying to the University of Phoenix, when I was in the United States Navy stationed in San Diego on shore duty (which means not attached to a ship). I gave The University of Phoenix a chance to win my tuition assistance money since military back then could get support for college, in the form of money for tuition. I met the University's representative back in 2004, and he explained to me since a single class was over $1000 to concentrate on a business degree; his solution was to use my Tuition Assistance and then dip into my G.I. Bill to cover the cost of the course. I am no math expert, but I thought to myself that the tuition was overpriced, especially when I get about $750 capped for a class. I would have had to use my extra benefits to cover the rest; on top of that I would have to pay for my books. I said "thank you, but no thank you." That is a ridiculous deal and they cannot justify their prices on tuition even though I had two forms of educational aid, imagine if I didn't?! Now visualize someone with no educational aid, possibly just a Pell grant and would have to be in a student loan which would be an outrageous amount to pay back, starting from the bottom to a 4 year degree. These people acted like it was the thing to do, which I'm sure they were full throttle after the great recession, since the amount of potential students grew significantly.

It is a shame that there are not many avenues that assist students, other than scholarships, grants and student aid (Pell grants). Of course, if you join the military, work for the school you are attending, or had parents utilize a 529 plan or something similar, then you would get a leg up in the degree plan. A lot of the populations that have ambitions to go to college don't really get to. As a whole, there are really not many students who can utilize that and will greatly impact the financial side of high education. The truth of the matter is, college has been getting extremely higher for people to afford, which most of the students currently have or will have to take a loan to support their tuition; which they think is normal.

So, if higher education was one of the cogs in the virtuous cycle, many students that graduate with degrees and go out into the working environment, land great paying jobs, which are free of student debt and could buy more things and pay more taxes. Wouldn't that be a start of a potentially productive economy? Let's say the department of education and the federal government cracked down and enforced the rules and regulations for not just the "for profit" schools but every college across the board, and then maybe we can count on a quality education with affordable tuition. So we all would not have to take out over priced loans with high interest rates. I believe, setting this industry up for success is a positive bet on our economy for the future.

Chapter 7
The Diminishing Rights and Privacy of the People

Truth is the rich and wealthy that run the market and industries doesn't really want us to have the rights and privileges that we currently enjoy. A society that is subservient to their masters will only drive the profits of the companies and corporations further and, in turn, will diminish more of our rights in an ongoing cycle because of their political and economic influences.

Since 9/11, the birth of the Patriot Act came about because of the terrorist attacks primarily in New York City and Washington D.C. that structured the diminishing cycle of our rights. Even though these laws are the very policies that are supposed to shield and protect the American citizens from terrorism foreign or domestically. There are no definitions of who is a terrorist, since everyone can potentially be a terrorist to the government and the NSA; they have to watch everyone for suspicious activity. Simply put, if someone suspects another person as a terrorist, then your rights as an American citizen are taken away.

So, to be clear, your rights to a fair trial, your rights to an unlawful detaining are gone; if there is enough evidence that supports you associating in terrorism and involved in a terrorist attack. It gets worse if you reside outside of the United States, since American forces can launch a missile from their many flying drones; if they deem someone is a potential threat. Even though many terrorist organizations are funded and supported by our so called allies such as Saudi Arabia, U.A.E, Iraq, and supposed potential new ally Iran, to name a few.

It is ridiculous, the amount of resources and efforts the government gives to the NSA to theoretically combat terrorism. According to the national priorities website, the current cost of fighting terrorism since 2001 is approximately 1.7 trillion dollars and every hour we are paying 8.36 million. Not sure about you but that's a heck of a lot of money to fight terrorism. You would think paying that amount of money would totally eradicate terrorism as a whole, but you would be surprised of what we do or don't do with the money.

A lot of funds and resources are spent to battle terrorism and it is generally through data and information collecting where the government collects: every phone call, every text and every internet inquiry to send to a huge data base to be sorted and processed. Under a program called PRISM the government can collect countless bits of information from the internet.

PRISM is a clandestine surveillance program, under which the United States National Security Agency (NSA) collects internet communications from at least nine major US internet companies. Since 2001, the United States government has increased its scope for such surveillance, and this program was launched in 2007.

PRISM is a government code name for a data-collection effort known officially by the SIGAD US-984XN. The PRISM program collects stored internet communications based on demands made to internet companies such as Google Inc. under Section 702 of the FISA Amendments Act of 2008; to turn over any data that match court-approved search terms. The NSA can use these PRISM requests to target communications that were encrypted when they traveled across the internet backbone, to focus on stored data that telecommunication filtering systems discarded earlier, and to get data that is easier to handle, among other things.

PRISM began in 2007 in the wake of the passage of the Protect America Act under the Bush Administration. The program is operated under the supervision of the U.S. Foreign Intelligence Surveillance Court (FISA Court, or FISC) pursuant to the Foreign Intelligence Surveillance Act (FISA). Its existence was leaked six years later by NSA contractor Edward Snowden, who warned that the extent of mass data collection was far greater than the public knew and included what he characterized as "dangerous" and "criminal" activities. The disclosures were published by The Guardian and The Washington Post on June 6, 2013. Subsequent documents have demonstrated a financial arrangement between NSA's Special Source Operations division (SSO) and PRISM partners in the millions of dollars.

Documents indicate that PRISM is "the number one source of raw intelligence used for NSA analytic reports", and it accounts for 91% of the NSA's internet traffic acquired under FISA section 702 authorities." The leaked information came to light one day after the revelation that the FISA Court had been ordering a subsidiary of telecommunications company, Verizon Communications, to turn over to the NSA logs tracking all of its customers' telephone calls.

U.S. government officials have disputed some aspects of the Guardian and Washington Post stories and have defended the program by asserting it: cannot be used on domestic targets without a warrant, that it has helped to prevent acts of terrorism, and that it receives independent oversight from the federal government's executive, judicial and legislative branches. On June 19, 2013, U.S. President Barack Obama, during a visit to Germany, stated that the NSA's data gathering practices constitute "a circumscribed, narrow system directed at us being able to protect our people."

PRISM was publicly revealed when classified documents about the program were leaked to journalists of The Washington Post and The Guardian by Edward Snowden – at the time a NSA contractor – during a visit to Hong Kong. The leaked documents included 41 PowerPoint slides, four of which were published in news articles. The documents identified several technology companies as participants in the PRISM program, including Microsoft in 2007, Yahoo! in 2008, Google in 2009, Facebook in 2009, Paltalk in 2009, YouTube in 2010, AOL in 2011, Skype in 2011 and Apple in 2012. The speaker's notes in the briefing document reviewed by The Washington Post indicated that "98 percent of PRISM production is based on Yahoo, Google, and Microsoft."

The information stated that much of the world's electronic communications pass through the U.S., because electronic communications data tend to follow the least expensive route rather than the most physically direct route, and the bulk of the world's internet infrastructure is based in the United States. The information noted that these facts provide United States intelligence analysts with opportunities for intercepting the communications of foreign targets as their electronic data pass into or through the United States.

Snowden's subsequent disclosures included statements that government agencies such as the United Kingdom's, GCHQ, also undertook mass interception and tracking of internet and communications data. It was described by Germany as "nightmarish" if true allegations that the NSA engaged in "dangerous" and "criminal" activity by "hacking" civilian infrastructure networks in other countries, such as "universities, hospitals, and private businesses." Alleged that compliance offered only very limited restrictive effect on mass data collection practices (including of Americans) since restrictions "are policy-based, not technically based, and can change at any time", adding that "Additionally, audits are cursory, incomplete, and easily fooled by fake justifications," with numerous self-granted exceptions, and that NSA policies encourage staff to assume the benefit of the doubt, in cases of uncertainty.

Edward Snowden is a known whistle blower that worked for the NSA and brought this program in the light of the public, sacrificing his career and citizenship in order to check the influence of the government's authority; its many different surveillance programs that in most cases infringe on our rights through very private means. Snowden summarized that "in general, the reality is this: if an NSA, FBI, CIA, DEA, etc. analyst has access to query raw SIGINT (signals intelligence) databases, they can enter and get results for anything they want."

According to The Washington Post, the intelligence analysts search PRISM data using terms intended to identify suspicious communications of targets whom the analysts suspect with at least 51 percent confidence to not be U.S. citizens. But in the process, communication data of some U.S. citizens are also collected unintentionally. Training materials for analysts tell them that while they should periodically report such accidental collection of non-foreign U.S. data, "it's nothing to worry about."

According to The Guardian, NSA had access to chats and emails on Hotmail.com and Skype, because Microsoft had "developed a surveillance capability to deal" with the interception of chats, and "for PRISM collection against Microsoft email services will be unaffected because PRISM collects this data prior to encryption."

Also, according to The Guardian's, Glenn Greenwald, even low-level NSA analysts are allowed to search and listen to the communications of Americans and other people without court approval and supervision. Greenwald said low level analysts can, via systems like PRISM, "listen to whatever emails they want, whatever telephone calls, browsing histories, Microsoft Word documents. And it's all done with no need to go to a court, with no need to even get supervisor approval on the part of the analyst."

He added that the NSA databank, with its years of collected communications, allows analysts to search that database and listen "to the calls or read the emails of everything that the NSA has stored, or look at the browsing histories or Google search terms that you've entered, and it also alerts them to any further activities that people connected to that email address or that IP address do in the future." Greenwald was referring in the context of the foregoing quotes to the NSA program X-Keyscore.

Shortly after publication of the reports by The Guardian and The Washington Post, the United States Director of National Intelligence, James Clapper, on June 7, 2013, released a statement confirming that for nearly six years the government of the United States had been using large internet services companies such as Facebook to collect information on foreigners outside the United States as a defense against national security threats. The statement read in part, "The Guardian and The Washington Post articles refer to collection of communications pursuant to Section 702 of the Foreign Intelligence Surveillance Act. They contain numerous inaccuracies." He went on to say, "Section 702 is a provision of FISA that is designed to facilitate the acquisition of foreign intelligence information concerning non-U.S. persons located outside the United States. It cannot be used to intentionally target any U.S. citizen, any other U.S. person, or anyone located within the United States." Clapper concluded his statement by stating, "The unauthorized disclosure of information about this important and entirely legal program is reprehensible and risks important protections for the security of Americans." On March 12, 2013, Clapper had told the United States Senate Select Committee on Intelligence that the NSA does "not wittingly" collect any type of data on millions or hundreds of millions of Americans. Clapper later admitted the statement he made on March 12, 2013, was a lie, or in his words, "I responded in what I thought was the most truthful, or least untruthful manner by saying no."

On June 7, 2013, U.S. President Barack Obama, referring to the PRISM program and the NSA's telephone calls logging program, said, "What you've got is two programs that were originally authorized by Congress, have been repeatedly authorized by Congress. Bipartisan majorities have approved them. Congress is continually briefed on how these are conducted. There are a whole range of safeguards involved and federal judges are overseeing the entire program throughout." He also said, "You can't have 100 percent security and then also have 100 percent privacy and zero inconvenience. You know, we're going to have to make some choices as a society." In separate statements, senior Obama administration officials (not mentioned by name in source) said that Congress had been briefed 13 times on the programs since 2009

The U.S. military has acknowledged blocking access to parts of The Guardian website for thousands of defense personnel across the country, and blocking the entire Guardian website for personnel stationed throughout Afghanistan, the Middle East, and South Asia. A spokesman said the military was filtering out reports and content relating to government surveillance programs to preserve "network hygiene" and prevent any classified material from appearing on unclassified parts of its computer systems. Access to the Washington Post, which also published information on classified NSA surveillance programs disclosed by Edward Snowden, had not been blocked at the time the blocking of access to The Guardian was reported.

So the question is, are they really protecting us when they are collecting all this data, and is this all really necessary? Why are they doing this all behind our backs?

Think about this in the explosion of cloud based services and massive storage servers. Why would the government not intrude in the information you send to these remote cloud based servers as well?! There is no reason why they wouldn't since it is easier to break into a remote sight and spy on your data instead of hacking into your personal computer, because your personal information is their already and available at these cloud base sites.

I understand that this is a really touchy subject and our rights are what weighs in the balance of these government surveillance programs that are supposed to protect the American citizens from terrorist activities. According to Edward Snowden, when he was being interviewed by HBO's VICE Shane Smith, he said that the government already has the ability to spy on our personal devices such as a smartphone, tablets, even a game device such as a PlayStation or XBOX since they have a camera and microphones attached, which are connected to the internet. That is even if you turn off your Wi-Fi setting and GPS, I believe they have sophisticated devices that will track your every move and record whatever you are doing no matter where you are.

Snowden demonstrated how to be surveillance free since each part of your phone is a separate component so each component can be hacked. The only way to know that you are not been hacked is to disconnect and or take out the camera and microphone. He stated that, "you bought the phone but the people that hacked into your phone actually own it" in every case that would be correct.

So it is at no surprise when the FBI requested that Apple give them the software to break into the San Bernardino terrorist iPhone, Apple would not comply. Their argument was if they can break into this phone who's to say they won't break into any other phones that would put their customer's privacies in jeopardy. And, of course, the FBI said, "Trust us, we won't do this to your customers," and thankfully Apple still did not comply. Unfortunately, the FBI connected with a third party tech company that made it happen anyway. So, basically the FBI won the battle but I think Apple won the war in the regards to privacy rights.

Regrettably, this is not the only issue we have with civil rights. The right to an assembly and petition has always been in jeopardy because of one reason or another. However, the power in numbers has influenced political decision making as long as the assembly is peaceful, but of course you see on the television assemblies that goes wrong and riot patrol is there with batons, riot shields and fire hoses when all hell breaks loose.

Along with our right to bear arms, a lot of people believe that we should not have any personal firearms to protect ourselves; we should rely on the government to handle that type of situation and freely give them the authority to protect us from all harm and danger. Well, if you are reading my book and came this far, I'm pretty sure you know my answer to that ridiculous theory. Now, as far as the laws that govern the right to bear arms, I believe that there are some gun loop-hole laws that criminals utilize and take advantage of to get their hand on fire arms. Such as "The gun show loophole" where anyone can purchase a gun at a gun show from a private seller and not have to go through a background check. I just think that this law is idiotic and should be closed immediately. Also, the fact that most background checks to purchase a firearm does not look into the mental history of the customer just the criminal record mostly needs to be looked as well.

So, the issue with the right to bear arms has a lot of push and pull, and because it is a touchy subject, the opposition on both sides is very prominent; since the opposition has groups like the NRA involved. The gun opposition can be cut down the middle of the Republican and Democratic parties. So you see where the friction lies concerning these types of rights issues and the gridlock it creates.

The basic rights that we live by and enjoy, are in fact, being chipped away one letter at a time; the fact that the government is utilizing every resource to survey and evaluate the information from everyone's phone, computer, and internet device, sets up the strategy of one governing entity (something like Big Brother but probably worse) with little to no rights for the people. Personally, if that happens, then that would create a place I would not want to live in or see my children grow up in, but unfortunately, that is the direction that our country is heading and many people know that, but do nothing about it for one reason or another.

Unfortunately, if the problem is not solved soon then the problem will solve us, and if the solution involves the deterioration of our civil rights then we as a society will suffer for that. The fact that we have whistle blowers, companies and people that take a stand and expose shady activities like the PRISM program will at least keep the government in line, instead of the people.

I would want to add, but it may be a bit off subject, but in some ways it's probably right with this chapter; there are other companies in the internet realm that are willfully taking our personal information when someone web searches and enters a website. These companies follow your internet surfing and links them with other companies such as Epsilon and many others to create a profile for you. They then sell it to other major companies or corporations to better understand and create a strategy that will make them more money; in the form of your purchases. But the fact that you don't even know they are doing this and are not willfully giving your data to you is very questionable.

Morgan Spurlock on his show, "The inside man," featuring privacy, actually went to one of these companies and personally asked them for his personal information that he knew they were gathering. The people that worked there basically treated Morgan like he was an intruder, made him wait quite a while and finally at one point they told him to leave. This was only after he talked to the manager at another facility, and basically assured him that everything was done legally and that they were "servicing the consumer." Wouldn't you think that a part of serving the consumer is to make them aware that they are being served? And you would actually give out the information upon request to these companies for the information being gathered and are holding for larger corporations or companies.

Of course you can "Opt-out" of these types of involuntary services for the consumer, but if you didn't know they were doing that behind your back then how are you supposed to know that you can opt-out of the involuntary tracking? There is a way to do this but it might take a lot of effort to get this completed, and that is how these internet tracking companies like it because the more difficult it is to do something the less likely someone will do it. Plus, the fact that they sell this information to companies that are constantly getting hacked into and records being lost, just like data breeches in Target, Experian and Neiman Marcus, the companies put millions of customers at risk; not properly securing this type of information. But of course, it is not their data that they are selling so it is not a priority for them. But it should be…

So, how is tied into the big scheme of the rich and powerful? I believe, that the more knowledge you have on someone and let's say this someone was your enemy, then the better you can understand to exploit their weaknesses and better take advantage of them and eventually conquer them. I believe this is another type of strategy that could be utilized by the rich to manipulate the public; since knowledge is power and for these companies the knowledge is unlimited now.

Chapter 8
The Secret Told

It is no surprise that the wealthy and powerful have influential tools at their disposal to further their agenda. But maybe most of you did not know is that they have secret meetings and rendezvous to ensure that they keep their money, influence and power. Many of the wealthy families sit down together to talk with a specialist in the field of finance, law or whatever the family might need to preserve their wealth and legacy.

This approach is obviously smart if you want your family to continually be successful and your wealth to last for generations; it would seem that more wealthy families are adopting or have adopted this type of strategy to further protect their riches. Of course, these families have the cash and influence to get the best type of services and planning money can buy, and they do get their money's worth.

The same can be said on a national and global scale, many rich and powerful put their differences aside and come together to create different strategies to win over certain issues and agendas. Take, for example, the Bilderberg group, this is an annual private conference of 120 to 150 people of the European and North American elite mostly, experts from industry, finance, academia, and the media, established in 1954.

The group's original goal of promoting Atlanticism, of strengthening US-European relations and preventing another world war; the Bilderberg Group's theme is to "bolster a consensus around free market Western capitalism and its interests around the globe" according to Andrew Kakabadse a professor at Henley Business School. In 2001, Denis Healey, a Bilderberg group founder and a steering committee member for 30 years, said, "To say we were striving for a one-world government is exaggerated, but not wholly unfair.

Those of us in Bilderberg felt we couldn't go on forever fighting one another for nothing, and killing people and rendering millions homeless. So, we felt that a single community throughout the world would be a good thing."

About two thirds of the participants come from Europe and the rest from North America; one third from politics and government and the rest from other fields. Historically, attendee lists have been weighted toward bankers, politicians, directors of large businesses and board members from large publicly traded corporations, including IBM, Xerox, Royal Dutch Shell, Nokia and Daimler. Heads of state, including former King Juan Carlos I of Spain and former Queen Beatrix of the Netherlands, have attended meetings. A source connected to the group told The Daily Telegraph in 2013, that other individuals, whose names are not publicly issued, sometimes turn up "just for the day" at the group's meetings.

Partly, because of its working methods to ensure strict privacy, the Bilderberg Group has been criticized for its lack of transparency and accountability. The undisclosed natures of the proceedings have given rise to several conspiracy theories. This outlook has been popular on both extremes of the political spectrum, even if they disagree about the exact nature of the group's intentions. Some on the left accuse the Bilderberg group of conspiring to impose capitalist domination, while some on the right have accused the group of conspiring to impose a world government and planned economy.

In 2005, Davignon discussed accusations of the group striving for a one-world government with the BBC: "It is unavoidable and it doesn't matter. There will always be people who believe in conspiracies but things happen in a much more incoherent fashion. … When people say this is a secret government of the world, I say that if we were a secret government of the world we should be bloody ashamed of ourselves."

In August 2010, former Cuban President, Fidel Castro, wrote a controversial article for the Cuban Communist Party newspaper Granma in which he cited Daniel Estulin's 2006 book, *"The Secrets of the Bilderberg Club,"* which, as quoted by Castro, describes, "sinister cliques and the Bilderberg lobbyists," manipulating the public, "to install a world government that knows no borders and is not accountable to anyone but its own self." Proponents of Bilderberg conspiracy theories in the United States include individuals and groups such as the John Birch Society, political activist Phyllis Schlafly, writer Jim Tucker, political activist Lyndon LaRouche, radio host Alex Jones, and politician Jesse Ventura, who made the Bilderberg group a topic of a 2009, episode of his TruTV series Conspiracy Theory with Jesse Ventura. Non-American proponents include Lithuanian writer Daniel Estulin.

Concerns about lobbying have arisen. Ian Richardson sees Bilderberg as the transnational power elite, "an integral, and to some extent critical, part of the existing system of global governance, that is, "not acting in the interests of the whole."

So, if there is any conspiracy about the rich extending their influence of power, this group would be a great example. But I'm certain that this is not the only group that gathers together and speaks of "important issue in our world's society" in private. It seems that their agenda is to integrate the world into one grouped government or power. This is talked about a lot in the Book of Revelations, if your faith leads you to believe the bible and its teachings.

The truth of the matter is, that all of the Bilderberg members are agreeing to confidentiality so we really do not know what actually goes on in these meeting; just speculation, unfortunately. But really, if we just used critical thinking about what goes on, I'm certain it is all about furthering the wealthy and rich agenda in many ways. Since powerful executives and board members of American and international companies and corporation are invited to these meeting, it's definitely not a summit to watch the flowers grow and sing Kumbaya.

There are many other meetings that our country participates and are involved in such as the G-8, and G-20 summit, for example. These types of assemblies have the press involved in every step every subject they talk about. So, it is not the fact that powerful people such as our president congregate and talk about global or domestic issues; it is the fact that some meeting such as the Bilderberg are closed off in a private setting and held confidentially.

These clandestine agenda meetings that are done in private could be the hammer that the walls of our society could be at the mercy of. Unfortunately, this is just one of possibly many secret groups meeting that goes on behind closed doors so that the public has no idea what is happening, in turn, cannot do anything to stop these potential egotistic agendas.

Do not get me wrong about the point of this chapter, and that is if the rich and wealthy had a great agenda for our world community; wouldn't you would think that they would somehow introduce these great ideas to us so that we all can revel in the information that is being shared. But of course, if you want to withhold information you must be private about the message and that is exactly what these members of these groups are demonstrating.

So again I bring up, why are they doing this? Just like the families that hold meetings to preserve their wealth and riches, so are these particular members of the gatherings and others that create a strategy to protect their wealth and status; at the same time producing a sub servient society that will bend to their every wish. Obviously, these members are very intelligent and the collective aptitude could make these particular individuals in these meetings very dangerous.

Chapter 9
The End Game

We all try to strive and improve in our lives and raise the quality of living for the most part. Achieving the "American Dream," should be the result of hard work and determination. This should be a true indicator of how much someone sacrifices to reach their goals and objectives in life.

That is why it is important to know these issues that plague our community, our society, our country and our world. I believe there is a sickness and it is manifesting from the inside, out. The amount of greed and selfishness that infests our government, which stems from the gluttonous rich and powerful and their counterparts, is one of the main causes of our problems, which seem to get worse as time passes on because no viable solution has been put into place.

From the executive compensation, the revolving door, to the increase in lobbying for the agenda of the rich and powerful, it is no surprise that there is gridlock in Washington where politicians rather go on vacation than to put in the time to pass a bill that will be beneficial to the American people. Not to mention the sequester (automatic spending cuts), which is the result of government shut down that shouldn't happen in the first place; direct result of politicians not doing their jobs.

This and the national debt will be a ticking time bomb that will eventually explode in everyone's face because nothing is being done to stop it or the fact that they are putting gasoline on the fire by further increasing our governments debt and deficit. Eventually, the tax payers and the population will again feel the effects of the self-inflicted economic suicide because our government can't afford their obligations which are stretching them too far.

So, if our leaders in Washington won't do anything to tackle our issues, then who will? Obviously, we elected politicians to work in the favor of the people in theory but the reality is that the majority is working for the rich and wealthy that lines their pockets with "contributions" among other benefits. But more and more working policies and bills that would benefit the people seems like a pipe dream instead of an obligation to the public.

It reminds me of another society that was its own demise and that was the Roman Empire, for almost 500 years the Roman Empire ruled the known world, conquering foreign territories and regions other empires could not overtake and rule. But in the last days of the empire, the authority figures did not function because of mass corruption and dysfunction which was plaguing the capital, in addition to a deteriorating economy. Many of the politicians sat on their hands and did nothing when the barbarians from the North basically walked in the front gate of the city of Rome and ransacked everything and everyone.

That is what split the empire in two and started the Holy Roman Empire to the West and the Byzantine Empire to the East. The empire was never the same after that which was a good lesson for other societies in the future like our country because history always seems to repeat itself. Yes, I know that times were different then and we have certain issues that the Roman Empire did not have back in the day, but I do believe history is repetitive and when certain issues are not handled properly in the right amount of time, it could be the difference from a thriving government or a government on the brink of collapse.

Corruption and class favoritism is never a good thing when it comes to the well-being of the public; this disease festers and grows until there is a decline of some sort as a result of lack of action and lack of support for the people.

Let's try to imagine a country that is too big and too corrupt, that not much is progressing and government services like our military have been significantly downsized because of budget issues and an induced depression of our economic system. Who's to say that a terrorist group or an international military force would take advantage of our weakness and just stroll into our borders and rage war on our lands because we have little to no forces to fight the invaders, just like the barbarians did in the Roman era. Of course, this is a hypothetical situation, but this is the direction I see us heading.

I think we are not confronting the issues that will manifest our lives, so if we do nothing to stop the <u>vicious cycle</u> and reverse the economic wheel to create a <u>virtuous cycle</u> for the benefit of everyone not only in our own country, but for other countries around the world, then I believe we are lost. Since our country is the leading economy in the world, our downfall will inevitably be their downfall of others internationally especially our allies. This is due to the fact that our dollar bill is the leading currency that the world uses because our money is supposedly solvent and is backed by a stable economy, but as I explained earlier, that the assumption in our currency and our sustainment of our economy will definitely change if there is another recession or depression. The confidence of the world looking to our countries economy will definitely inverse and, in turn, will change the perception of our money being the lead currency in the world's monetary system. This is what created the Bit coin block chain system, due to the lack of trust in our economy.

Some international countries such as China, Germany and Russia have already been bringing up these economic points and issues; if there is an economic fall then there is probably going to have to switch from the American dollar standard to something different like block chain crypto currencies. So, if this happens, then we are in trouble, because the confidence of our economy is thoroughly tied into every major country that has a trade agreement with us or relies on our country for vital goods, support and services.

Just like the consumer confidence that has gone away or is stagnate, our economy because there is no spending, so will the confidence of other countries deteriorate the perception of our trade and Gross Domestic Product in the world economy stage. And talking about how fragile the world economy is, definitely is an understatement, and if a catastrophe like a depression of our economy happens then the rest of the world will follow like a house of cards, blowing in the wind.

It really is a horrible situation when you think about it, And if this disaster happens then what? Is the world going to have to file for bankruptcy? Not exactly, but the scenario will set up for a new world currency system, whatever that would be. Who knows, there might be a situation where depending on the outcome of the event will possibly create a new unified exchange that could be regional or global; that would possibly fulfill the Bilderberg conspiracies.

I hope, by reading this book, I did not preach too much doom and gloom, but actually put out the important information and specifics that suppress our society and keep our economy from reaching new heights because of someone's agenda to hoard the riches. I personally, listen to people that think outside of the box about the economy and try to create viable solutions to prosper in this economic stage. People such as Robert Kiyosaki, Dave Ramsey, and Robert Reich to name a few that have different theories or principle that the middle to low class can understand and implement. I believe the more you understand the issues and create a long lasting solution, the more we can make a potential change that will benefit all; not just the rich and powerful.

I don't necessarily consider myself to be an economic expert, but by listening and observing different patterns and movements in the market and in the economy, you get the consensus of certain issues as a whole and what is done or not done to better the economy. I just hope that my objective in creating awareness in this particular subject doesn't create a sense of pessimism in our leadership and lack of allegiance to our nation, but build an awareness to overcome these types of economy and financial issues. To better our lives and the lives of our families that will filter down through generations.

Bliss Factor Research Sources

Cowspiracy: The Sustainability Secret

http://fedupmovie.com

https://www.nationalpriorities.org/cost-of

http://money.cnn.com/2015/02/03/pf/college/corinthian-college-student-debt/index.html

https://en.wikipedia.org/wiki/PRISM

https://en.wikipedia.org/wiki/Bilderberg_Group

https://projects.propublica.org/bailout/list

http://www.thezeitgeistmovement.com

https://www.opensecrets.org/revolving

https://en.wikipedia.org/wiki/Revolving_door_(Politics)

http://www.accountingweb.com/aa/law-and-enforcement/us-ceo-compensation-abuse-or-reward

https://en.wikipedia.org/wiki/Executive_compensation

www.ingramcontent.com/pod-product-compliance
Lightning Source LLC
Chambersburg PA
CBHW030010190526
45157CB00014B/2035